Rabbit Poems

21 CLASSIC POEMS ABOUT
RABBITS, BUNNIES & HARES

Contents

The Rabbit *Elizabeth Madox Roberts*	 1
The Hare and the Tortoise *Jean de la Fontaine*	 3
Ballad of the Lost Hare *Margaret Sidney*	 7
The Tale of Tails *Arthur Guiterman*	 17
Mending Wall *Robert Frost*	 21
The Hare *Walter de la Mare*	 25
Mariana in the North *V. Sackville-West*	 27
The Persevering Tortoise and the Pretentious Hare *Guy Wetmore Carryl*	 29
Hares at Play *John Clare*	 33
Ballad for Bishops *Lord Alfred Douglas*	 35

The Black Cat

The Hare 39
  Wilfrid Wilson Gibson

The Hare's Ears 53
  Jean de la Fontaine

Night Fall in the Ti-Tree 55
  Geraldine Rede and Violet Teague

Song in Autumn 59
  Djuna Barnes

The Town Rabbit in the Country 61
  Camilla Doyle

Gathering Leaves 65
  Robert Frost

Epitaph on a Hare 67
  William Cowper

On Seeing a Wounded Hare Limp by Me, ... 71
Which a Fellow Had Just Shot At
  Robert Burns

Resolution and Independence 73
  William Wordsworth

The Hare and the Frogs 79
  Jean de la Fontaine

The Easter Bunny 83
  M. Josephine Todd

The Rabbit
by Elizabeth Madox Roberts

When they said the time to hide was mine,
I hid back under a thick grape vine.

And while I was still for the time to pass,
A little gray thing came out of the grass.

He hopped his way through the melon bed
And sat down close by a cabbage head.

He sat down close where I could see,
And his big still eyes looked hard at me,

His big eyes bursting out of the rim,
And I looked back very hard at him.

The Hare and the Tortoise
by Jean de la Fontaine

It's not enough that you run fleet;
Start early,—that's the way to beat.

The Tortoise said unto the Hare,
"I'll bet you, free, and frank, and fair,
You do not reach a certain place
So soon as I, though quick your pace."
"So soon?" the nimble creature cries;
"Take physic for your brains;—be wise"—
"Fool or no fool, I make the bet."
The bet is made, the stakes are set;
But who the sporting judges were
Is neither your nor my affair.
Our Hare had but a bound to make,
From him the swiftest hounds to shake.
They run themselves almost to death,
Yet he is scarcely out of breath;
Plenty of time for him to browse,
To sleep, and then again to rouse;
Or boldly turn the while he's going,
And mark which way the wind is blowing.
Careless, he lets the Tortoise pace,
Grave as a senator. To race
With such a thing is but disgrace.
She, in the meanwhile, strives and strains,
And takes most meritorious pains;
Slow, yet unceasing. Still the Hare
Holds it a very mean affair
To start too soon; but when, at last,

The winning-post is almost past
By his dull rival, then, 'tis true,
He quicker than the arrow flew.
Alas! his efforts failed to win,
The Tortoise came the first one in.
"Well," she said then, "now, was I right?
What use was all your swiftness: light
I held your speed, and won the prize;
Where would you be, can you surmise,
If with my house upon your shoulders,
You tried to startle all beholders?"

Ballad of the Lost Hare
by Margaret Sidney

INTRODUCTION.

I.

Far from wild,
Far from wood,
In a field
Rich and good;

II.

Near to hill,
And winding glade,
Lived the naughtiest
Hare e'er made.

III.

Father scolded,
Mother whipped,
But every day
Away he slipped.

IV.

Brothers three,
And sisters two,
Cried and cried
As off he flew.

V.

Sore—sore—sore was the sobbing,
Wild—wild—wild was his race;
Only the woods to echo his footsteps,
Only the winds—his hiding-place.

VI.

Once he fled,
Twice he fled,
Over meadow
And garden bed.

VII.

Thrice he had
The rarest fun,
Fourth was just
Another one.

VIII.

Mad the races,
Jolly the Hare,
Little did he
Reck or care.

IX.

The winds might blow,
The waters flow,
Over the hills
Away he'd go!

X.

"Don't you come home," the father said,
"Until you can stay in your little bed;
One more race and you keep away,
Though you should beg and cry all day."

XI.

Alack!
He never came back;
That swift-footed Hare,
That knowing Hare,
That beast who didn't
Reck nor care.
Whether swallowed alive,
Or hung on a rail,
Or dancing along
The waters pale,
Or running, or walking,
Or leaping a star,
He was gone so long,
And he went so far,
That the winds forgot
His very name;
And lost to memory,
Love, and fame,
He became in verity
The LOST HARE!

ADVENTURES.

Little Bossy Whitefoot
Grazing in a field,
Eating all the green grass,
Such a tender yield;
Dreaming of the days,
When she would be a cow,
How she wished that very time
Would come just now.

She shook her frisky feet,
And wrinkled up her nose,
And tossed her pretty head,
Then trotted on her toes.
When—looking down, she saw
Two frightened eyes,
And there the Hare and Bossy stood
In mutual surprise!

"I'm sorry I have scared you,"
Said this Hare considerate,
"Good bye, I must be going,
For it is very late."
He turned him on his long legs,
He scuttled thro' the glade,
He held his head as if, forsooth,
HE never were afraid!

The next he knew, with accent bold,
A dread voice cried—"Intruder—HOLD!"

"I'll butt you," cried a Goat,
"If you don't get off my rock."

The Hare could scarcely breathe,
So frightful was the shock.
He gasped; he tried to utter
A word with meaning fraught,
But to save his neck he couldn't
Control a single thought.

The Goat was tired of waiting,
He started for the Hare,
Only to find a vacant place,
Only to stand and stare.
For a flash of flying feet,
A glimpse of a gleaming eye,
Was all that marked this Hero,
Who'd rather run than die.

And now a neigh and a snort tremendous,
Aroused an echo most stupendous!

A Mustang gay,
A Mustang free,
Looked at the little Hare
Carelessly.
Looked—then curvetted,
Inviting to play,
But the Hare almost trembled,
Its life away.

"No—No—No!" he cried,
In wild protesting,
"I haven't come for play,
Nor any jesting."
"Ha—Ha!" laughed the Mustang,
And then "Hey? Hey?"

And kicking up his heels,
He began to neigh.

The Hare stole off,
In fact, he RAN
As he hadn't run before
From beast or man.
He tucked under fences,
He skipped around trees,
He didn't pause to take a look,
Or even stop to sneeze.

When a horrible bellow,
A wheeze and a snort
Came close to his ears
With loudest report
And a Bull most furious,
With rage not spurious,
Dashed up with a curious
Bow and a stare.

Little Hare panting—
Angry Bull ranting—
Ah—what a race!
Oh, and he'll catch him,
Then he'll despatch him,
Pitiful chase!

'Twas a hair-breadth escape—I tell you true!
I'd have given a dime to have been there in time
To see them sweep by—those two!

Three little Lambs
Playing in clover
Called to the frightened Hare

Over and over.
"Come with us—into this
Pretty, pretty spot?"

Gasped he flying past,
"I'd—rather—not!"
"RATHER NOT, INDEED!"
Each Lamb rubbed his eye,
Then stared in calm disdain,
To see him onward fly.

"He may"—then all exclaimed
In accents terse,
"Go further if he cares,
And fare much worse."

Whish—whirr! on his track
Fast at his heels comes a flying pack!
Baying, snapping,
Howling, yelling!
Can he get away?
There is no telling!

Fly little swift feet over dale and hill,
Take him dashing, flashing by the mill;
Tips of his toes, twinkle, twinkle fast,
Don't let the dogs eat him up at last!

Don't let the hungry, cruel, cruel jaws
Snap off his pretty little velvet paws,
Tear off his ears in terrible sport—
DON'T let the naughty little thing be caught!

Ah!
A hole—a hole!

In he goes!
The dogs tumble up
To stare at his toes.

They gnash their jaws,
And bewail their fate;
But to eat little Hare
Must wait—must wait!

CONCLUSION.

Had ever a beast such mad career?
Such a hare-brained race,
Such a long, long chase,
As this silly little Hare recorded here?

This Hare, who wouldn't stop to fight,
Who ran away both day and night
Who put himself delightedly
Among the best of company,

Who acting soon a reckless part,
Then posted off with all his heart;
Forever he's compelled to roam,
He never can enjoy a home.

Hark! do you think that's rustling wind?
Oh no, its nothing of the kind;
It's this poor, homeless, restless Hare
Rushing here, there, and everywhere.

List! do you hear the rain-drops fall
In gentle shower from tree-top tall?

Oh me!
Oh my!
It's poor Hare pattering by.

By the light of the silver moon—moon—moon,
He runs to the rhythm of a dismal tune;
In the gay merry shine of a summer day,
He still is running, away—away.

In cold, in heat, in rain, in snow,
This poor little creature must go—must go;
Perhaps if you're there in time you'll see
This wandering Hare,
This miserable Hare,
Rush over the hill-top, bleak and bare.

Do you suppose he wishes his home to see,
His sisters two, and his brothers three?
Would he like to lie down in his own little bed?
And does he recall what his father said?

And long for his mother to tuck him up tight,
Just as she used to, every night?
Who can say
As alway
He goes on—and on—and on—and on——

The Tale of Tails
by Arthur Guiterman

In unrecorded ages when the minnows talked like whales,
the very-clever-animals were destitute of tails:
The Monkey and the 'possum couldn't hang 'emselves to dry,
the puppy couldn't waggle, nor the Heifer flap a fly;
So when the wild geese trumpeted that tails could soon be had,
the very-clever-animals were very, very' glad.

Upon the day appointed, when the quadrupedal rout
were flocking to the trysting-place-where-tails-were-given-out,
The gnowley bear was settling to his wonted winter nap;
He called his friend, the rabbit, an obliging little chap,
And pledged him by the whiskers of the grate ancestral hare
To fetch a fitting tail-piece for a self-respecting bear.

But where the teils were given, there was such a dreadful crush—
A mingled game of football and a bargain-counter rush—
That bunny, hopping wildly for his own desired end,
Forgot his solemn promise to his sleepy-headed friend!

The rabbit was returning to his merry native vale,
Rejoicing in the flourish of a lovely, furry tail,
When, rapidly descending from his rocky mountain lair,
He saw the massive figure of his friend, the growly bear,
who roared, "My tail, o rabbit! Let me have it on the spot!"
"Why—" stammered out the rabbit, "please excuse me, —
I forgot!"

Oh, bruin swung his forepaw like a mighty iron flail;
He smote our luckless bunny on the precious furry tail
And shore it off completely, save a little bit of fluff!—
Still, honey, for a bunny that is cotton-tail enough.

Mending Wall
by Robert Frost

Something there is that doesn't love a wall,
That sends the frozen-ground-swell under it,
And spills the upper boulders in the sun;
And makes gaps even two can pass abreast.
The work of hunters is another thing:
I have come after them and made repair
Where they have left not one stone on a stone,
But they would have the rabbit out of hiding,
To please the yelping dogs. The gaps I mean,
No one has seen them made or heard them made,
But at spring mending-time we find them there.
I let my neighbor know beyond the hill;
And on a day we meet to walk the line
And set the wall between us once again.
We keep the wall between us as we go.
To each the boulders that have fallen to each.
And some are loaves and some so nearly balls
We have to use a spell to make them balance:
"Stay where you are until our backs are turned!"
We wear our fingers rough with handling them.
Oh, just another kind of outdoor game,
One on a side. It comes to little more:
There where it is we do not need the wall:
He is all pine and I am apple orchard.
My apple trees will never get across
And eat the cones under his pines, I tell him.
He only says, "Good fences make good neighbors."
Spring is the mischief in me, and I wonder
If I could put a notion in his head:

"Why do they make good neighbors? Isn't it
Where there are cows? But here there are no cows.
Before I built a wall I'd ask to know
What I was walling in or walling out,
And to whom I was like to give offense.
Something there is that doesn't love a wall,
That wants it down." I could say "Elves" to him,
But it's not elves exactly, and I'd rather
He said it for himself. I see him there
Bringing a stone grasped firmly by the top
In each hand, like an old-stone savage armed.
He moves in darkness as it seems to me,
Not of woods only and the shade of trees.
He will not go behind his father's saying,
And he likes having thought of it so well
He says again, "Good fences make good neighbors."

The Hare
by Walter de la Mare

In the black furrow of a field
I saw an old witch-hare this night;
And she cocked a lissome ear,
And she eyed the moon so bright,
And she nibbled o' the green;
And I whispered "Whsst! witch-hare",
Away like a ghostie o'er the field
She fled, and left the moonlight there.

Mariana in the North
by V. Sackville-West

All her youth is gone, her beautiful youth outworn,
Daughter of tarn and tor, the moors that were once her home
No longer know her step on the upland tracks forlorn
Where she was wont to roam.

All her hounds are dead, her beautiful hounds are dead,
That paced beside the hoofs of her high and nimble horse,
Or streaked in lean pursuit of the tawny hare that fled
Out of the yellow gorse.

All her lovers have passed, her beautiful lovers have passed,
The young and eager men that fought for her arrogant hand,
And the only voice which endures to mourn for her at the last
Is the voice of the lonely land.

The Persevering Tortoise and the Pretentious Hare
by Guy Wetmore Carryl

Once a turtle, finding plenty
In seclusion to bewitch,
Lived a *dolce far niente*
Kind of life within a ditch;
Rivers had no charm for him,
As he told his wife and daughter,
"Though my friends are in the swim,
Mud is thicker far than water."

One fine day, as was his habit,
He was dozing in the sun,
When a young and flippant rabbit
Happened by the ditch to run:
"Come and race me," he exclaimed,
"Fat inhabitant of puddles.
Sluggard! You should be ashamed.
Such a life the brain befuddles."

This, of course, was banter merely,
But it stirred the torpid blood
Of the turtle, and severely
Forth he issued from the mud.
"Done!" he cried. The race began,
But the hare resumed his banter,
Seeing how his rival ran
In a most unlovely canter.

Shouting, "Terrapin, you're bested!
You'd be wiser, dear old chap,
If you sat you down and rested
When you reach the second lap."
Quoth the turtle, "I refuse.
As for you, with all your talking,
Sit on any lap you choose.
I shall simply go on walking."

Now this sporting proposition
Was, upon its face, absurd;
Yet the hare, with expedition,
Took the tortoise at his word,
Ran until the final lap,
Then, supposing he'd outclassed him,
Laid him down and took a nap
And the patient turtle passed him!

Plodding on, he shortly made the
Line that marked the victor's goal;
Paused, and found he'd won, and laid the
Flattering unction to his soul.
Then in fashion grandiose,
Like an after-dinner speaker,
Touched his flipper to his nose,
And remarked, "Ahem! Eureka!"

And THE MORAL (lest you miss one)
Is: There's often time to spare,
And that races are (like this one)
Won not always by a hair.

Hares at Play
by John Clare

The birds are gone to bed, the cows are still,
And sheep lie panting on each old mole-hill;
And underneath the willow's gray-green bough,
Like toil a-resting, lies the fallow plough.
The timid hares throw daylight fears away
On the lane's road to dust and dance and play,
Then dabble in the grain by naught deterred
To lick the dew-fall from the barley's beard;
Then out they sturt again and round the hill
Like happy thoughts dance, squat, and loiter still,
Till milking maidens in the early morn
Jingle their yokes and sturt them in the corn;
Through well-known beaten paths each nimbling hare
Sturts quick as fear, and seeks its hidden lair.

Ballad for Bishops
by Lord Alfred Douglas

BISHOPS and others who inhabit
The mansions of the blest on earth,
Grieved by decline of infant birth,
Have drawn attention to the rabbit.
Not by design these good men work
To raise that beast to heights contested,
But by comparison, suggested,
With those who procreation shirk.

For if a nation's moral status
Be measured by prolific habit,
Between man and the meanest rabbit
There is an evident hiatus.

Each year, by lowest computations,
Six times the rabbit rears her young,
And frequent marriages among
The very closest blood relations
In very tender years ensure
A constant stream of "little strangers,"
Who, quickly grown to gallant rangers,
See that their families endure.

Not theirs to shirk paternal cares,
Moved by considerations sordid,
A child can always "be afforded";
The same applies to Belgian hares.

These noble brutes, pure Duty's pendants,
May live to see their blood vermilion
Coursing through something like a billion
Wholly legitimate descendants.

Knowledge's path is hard and stony,
And some may read who unaware are
That rabbit brown and Belgian hare are
Both members of the genus Coney.

The common hare, who lives in fields
And never goes into a hole,
(In this inferior to the mole)
In all things to the Belgian yields.

He will, immoral brute, decline
To multiply domestic "pledges,"
The family he rears in hedges
Is often limited to nine.

Such shocking want of *savoir faire,*
(Surely a symptom of insanity)
Might goad a Bishop to profanity
Were it not for the Belgian hare.

The Hare
by Wilfrid Wilson Gibson

My hands were hot upon a hare,
Half-strangled, struggling in a snare—
My knuckles at her warm wind-pipe—
When suddenly, her eyes shot back,
Big, fearful, staggering and black:
And, ere I knew, my grip was slack;
And I was clutching empty air,
Half-mad, half-glad at my lost luck ...
When I awoke beside the stack.

'Twas just the minute when the snipe,
As though clock-wakened, every jack,
An hour ere dawn, dart in and out
The mist-wreaths filling syke and slack,
And flutter wheeling round about,
And drumming out the Summer night.
I lay star-gazing yet a bit:
Then, chilly-skinned, I sat upright,
To shrug the shivers from my back:
And, drawing out a straw to suck,
My teeth nipped through it at a bite ...
The liveliest lad is out of pluck
An hour ere dawn—a tame cock-sparrow—
When cold stars shiver through his marrow,
And wet mist soaks his mother-wit.

But, as the snipe dropped, one by one;
And one by one the stars blinked out;
I knew 'twould only need the sun

To send the shudders right about:
And, as the clear East faded white,
I watched and wearied for the sun—
The jolly, welcome, friendly sun—
The sleepy sluggard of a sun
That still kept snoozing out of sight,
Though well he knew the night was done . . .
And, after all, he caught me dozing;
And leapt up, laughing, in the sky
Just as my lazy eyes were closing:
And it was good as gold to lie
Full-length among the straw, and feel
The day wax warmer every minute,
As, glowing glad, from head to heel,
I soaked and rolled rejoicing in it . . .
When from the corner of my eye,
Upon a heathery knowe hard-by,
With long lugs cocked, and eyes astare,
Yet all serene, I saw a hare.

Upon my belly in the straw,
I lay, and watched her sleek her fur,
As, daintily, with well-licked paw,
She washed her face and neck and ears:
Then, clean and comely in the sun,
She kicked her heels up, full of fun,
As if she did not care a pin
Though she should jump out of her skin;
And leapt and lolloped, free of fears,
Until my heart frisked round with her.
"And yet, if I but lift my head,
You'll scamper off, young Puss," I said.
"Still, I can't lie, and watch you play
Upon my belly half-the-day.

The Lord alone knows where I'm going:
But, I had best be getting there.
Last night I loosed you from the snare—
Asleep, or waking, who's for knowing!—
So, I shall thank you now for showing
Which art to take to bring me where
My luck awaits me. When you're ready
To start, I'll follow on your track.
Though slow of foot, I'm sure and steady . . ."
She pricked her ears, then set them back;
And like a shot was out of sight:
And, with a happy heart and light
As quickly I was on my feet;
And following the way she went,
Keen as a lurcher on the scent,
Across the heather and the bent,
Across the quaking moss and peat.
Of course, I lost her soon enough;
For moorland tracks are steep and rough;
And hares are made of nimbler stuff
Than any lad of seventeen,
However lanky-legged and tough,
However, kestrel-eyed and keen:
And I'd at last to stop and eat
The little bit of bread and meat
Left in my pocket overnight.
So, in a hollow, snug and green,
I sat beside a burn, and dipped
The dry bread in an icy pool;
And munched a breakfast fresh and cool . . .
And then sat gaping like a fool . . .
For, right before my very eyes,
With lugs acock, and eyes astare,
I saw again the selfsame hare.

So, up I jumped, and off she slipped:
And I kept sight of her until
I stumbled in a hole, and tripped;
And came a heavy, headlong spill:
And she, ere I'd the wit to rise,
Was o'er the hill, and out of sight:
And, sore and shaken with the tumbling,
And sicker at my foot for stumbling,
I cursed my luck, and went on, grumbling
The way her flying heels had fled.

The sky was cloudless overhead;
And just alive with larks asinging:
And, in a twinkling, I was swinging
Across the windy hills, lighthearted.
A kestrel at my footstep started,
Just pouncing on a frightened mouse,
And hung o'erhead with wings a-hover:
Through rustling heath an adder darted:
A hundred rabbits bobbed to cover:
A weasel, sleek and rusty-red,
Popped out of sight as quick as winking:
I saw a grizzled vixen slinking
Behind a clucking brood of grouse
That rose and cackled at my coming:
And all about my way were flying
The peewit, with their slow wings creaking:
And little jack-snipe darted, drumming:
And now and then a golden plover
Or redshank piped with reedy whistle.
But never shaken bent or thistle
Betrayed the quarry I was seeking
And not an instant, any where
Did I clap eyes upon a hare.

So, travelling still, the twilight caught me:
And as I stumbled on, I muttered:
"A deal of luck the hare has brought me!
The wind and I must spend together
A hungry night among the heather.
If I'd her here . . ." And as I uttered,
I tripped, and heard a frightened squeal;
And dropped my hands in time to feel
The hare just bolting 'twixt my feet.
She slipped my clutch: and I stood there,
And cursed that devil-littered hare,

That left me stranded in the dark
In that wide waste of quaggy peat,
Beneath black night without a spark:
When, looking up, I saw a flare
Upon a far-off hill, and said:
"By God, the heather is afire!
It's mischief at this time of year . . ."
And then, as one bright flame shot higher,
And booths and vans stood out quite clear;
My wits came back into my head:
And I remembered Brough Hill Fair.
And, as I stumbled towards the glare,
I knew the sudden kindling meant
The Fair was over for the day;
And all the cattle-folk away
And gipsy-folk and tinkers now
Were lighting supper-fires without
Each caravan and booth and tent.
And, as I climbed the stiff hill-brow,
I quite forgot my lucky hare.
I'd something else to think about:
For well I knew there's broken meat

For empty bellies after fair-time;
And looked to have a royal rare time
With something rich and prime to eat:
And then to lie and toast my feet
All night beside the biggest fire.

But, even as I neared the first,
A pleasant whiff of stewing burst
From out a smoking pot a-bubble:
And, as I stopped behind the folk
Who sprawled around, and watched it seething;
A woman heard my eager breathing,
And, turning, caught my hungry eye:
And called out to me: "Draw in nigher,
Unless you find it too much trouble;
Or you've a nose for better fare,
And go to supper with the Squire . . .
You've got the hungry parson's air!"
And all looked up, and took the joke,
As I dropped gladly to the ground
Among them, where they all lay gazing
Upon the bubbling and the blazing.
My eyes were dazzled by the fire
At first; and then I glanced around;
And, in those swarthy, fire-lit faces—
Though drowsing in the glare and heat
And snuffing the warm savour in,
Dead-certain of their fill of meat—
I felt the bit between the teeth,
The flying heels, the broken traces,
And heard the highroad ring beneath
The trampling hoofs: and knew them kin.
Then for the first time, standing there
Behind the woman who had hailed me,

I saw a girl with eyes astare
That looked in terror o'er my head:
And, all at once, my courage failed me . . .
For now again, and sore-adread,
My hands were hot upon a hare,
That struggled, strangling in the snare . . .
Then once more as the girl stood clear,
Before me--quaking cold with fear
I saw the hare look from her eyes . . .

And when, at last, I turned to see
What held her scared, I saw a man—
A fat man with dull eyes aleer—
Within the shadow of the van:
And I was on the point to rise
To send him spinning 'mid the wheels,
And twist his neck between his heels,
And stop his leering grin with mud . . .
And would have done it in a tick . . .
When, suddenly, alive with fright,
She started, with red, parted lips,
As though she guessed we'd come to grips,
And turned her black eyes full on me . . .
And, as I looked into their light,
My heart forgot the lust of fight,
And something shot me to the quick,
And ran like wildfire through my blood,
And tingled to my finger-tips . . .
And, in a dazzling flash, I knew
I'd never been alive before . . .
And she was mine for evermore.

While all the others slept asnore
In caravan and tent that night,

I lay alone beside the fire;
And stared into its blazing core,
With eyes that would not shut or tire,
Because the best of all was true,
And they looked still into the light
Of her eyes, burning ever bright.
Within the brightest coal for me ...
Once more, I saw her, as she started,
And glanced at me with red lips parted:
And, as she looked, the frightened hare

Had fled her eyes; and, merrily,
She smiled, with fine teeth flashing white,
As though she, too, were happy-hearted ...
Then she had trembled suddenly,
And dropped her eyes, as that fat man
Stepped from the shadow of the van,
And joined the circle, as the pot
Was lifted off, and, piping-hot,
The supper steamed in wooden bowls.
Yet, she had hardly touched a bite:
And never raised her eyes all night
To mine again: but on the coals,
As I sat staring, she had stared—
The black curls, shining round her head
From under the red kerchief, tied
So nattily beneath her chin—
And she had stolen off to bed
Quite early, looking dazed and scared.
Then, all agape and sleepy-eyed,
Ere long the others had turned in:
And I was rid of that fat man,
Who slouched away to his own van.

And now, before her van, I lay,
With sleepless eyes, awaiting day:
And, as I gazed upon the glare,
I heard, behind, a gentle stir:
And, turning round, I looked on her
Where she stood on the little stair
Outside the van, with listening air—
And, in her eyes, the hunted hare . . .
And then, I saw her slip away,
A bundle underneath her arm,
Without a single glance at me.
I lay a moment wondering,
My heart a-thump like anything,
Then, fearing she should come to harm,
I rose, and followed speedily
Where she had vanished in the night.
And, as she heard my step behind,
She started, and stopt dead with fright:
Then blundered on as if struck blind:
And now as I caught up with her,
Just as she took the moorland track,
I saw the hare's eyes, big and black . . .
She made as though she'd double back . . .
But, when she looked into my eyes,
She stood quite still and did not stir . . .
And, picking up her fallen pack,
I tucked it 'neath my arm; and she
Just took her luck quite quietly.
As she must take what chance might come,
And would not have it otherwise,
And walked into the night with me,
Without a word across the fells.

And, all about us, through the night,
The mists were stealing, cold and white,
Down every rushy syke or slack:

But, soon the moon swung into sight;
And, as we went, my heart was light,
And singing like a burn in flood:
And in my ears were tinkling bells:
My body was a rattled drum:
And fifes were shrilling through my blood
That summer night, to think that she
Was walking through the world with me.

But when the air with dawn was chill,
As we were travelling down a hill,
She broke her silence with low-sobbing:
And told her tale, her bosom throbbing
As though her very heart were shaken
With fear she'd yet be overtaken ...
She'd always lived in caravans—

Her father's, gay as any man's,
Grass-green, picked out with red and yellow,
And glittering brave with burnished brass
That sparkled in the sun like flame,
And window curtains, white as snow ...
But, they had died, ten years ago,
Her parents both, when fever came ...
And they were buried, side by side,
Somewhere beneath the wayside grass ...
In times of sickness, they kept wide
Of towns and busybodies, so
No parson's or policeman's tricks
Should bother them when in a fix ...
Her father never could abide
A black coat or a blue, poor man ...
And so, Long Dick, a kindly fellow,
When you could keep him from the can,

And Meg, his easy-going wife,
Had taken her into their van;
And kept her since her parents died . . .
And she had lived a happy life,
Until Fat Pete's young wife was taken . . .
But, ever since, he'd pestered her . . .
And she dared scarcely breathe or stir,
Lest she should see his eyes aleer . . .
And many a night she'd lain and shaken,
And very nearly died of fear—
Though safe enough within the van
With Mother Meg and her good-man—
For, since Fat Pete was Long Dick's friend,
And they were thick and sweet as honey;
And Dick owed Pete a pot of money,
She knew too well how it must end . . .
And she would rather lie stone dead
Beneath the wayside grass than wed
With leering Pete, and live the life,
And die the death, of his first wife . . .
And so, last night, clean-daft with dread,
She'd bundled up a pack and fled . . .

When all the sobbing tale was out,
She dried her eyes, and looked about,
As though she'd left all fear behind,
And out of sight were out of mind.
Then, when the dawn was burning red,
"I'm hungry as a hawk!" she said:
And from the bundle took out bread.
And, at the happy end of night,
We sat together by a burn:
And ate a thick slice, turn by turn;
And laughed and kissed between each bite.

Then, up again, and on our way
We went; and tramped the livelong day
The moorland trackways, steep and rough,
Though there was little fear enough
That they would follow on our flight.
And then again a shiny night
Among the honey-scented heather,
We wandered in the moonblaze bright,
Together through a land of light,
A lad and lass alone with life.
And merrily we laughed together,
When, starting up from sleep, we heard
The cock-grouse talking to his wife . . .
And "Old Fat Pete" she called the bird.

Six months and more have cantered by:
And, Winter past, we're out again—
We've left the fat and weather-wise
To keep their coops and reeking sties,
And eat their fill of oven-pies,
While we win free and out again

To take potluck beneath the sky
With sun and moon and wind and rain.
Six happy months . . . and yet, at night,
I've often wakened in affright,
And looked upon her lying there,
Beside me sleeping quietly,
Adread that when she waked, I'd see
The hunted hare within her eyes.

And, only last night, as I slept
Beneath the shelter of a stack . . .
My hands were hot upon a hare,

Half-strangled, struggling in the snare,
When, suddenly, her eyes shot back,
Big, fearful, staggering and black;
And ere I knew, my grip was slack,
And I was clutching empty air . . .
Bolt-upright from my sleep I leapt . . .
Her place was empty in the straw . . .
And then, with quaking heart, I saw
That she was standing in the night,
A leveret cuddled to her breast . . .

I spoke no word: but, as the light
Through banks of Eastern cloud was breaking,
She turned, and saw that I was waking:
And told me how she could not rest;
And, rising in the night, she'd found
This baby-hare crouched on the ground;
And she had nursed it quite a while:
But, now, she'd better let it go . . .
Its mother would be fretting so . . .
A mother's heart . . .
                I saw her smile,
And look at me with tender eyes:
And as I looked into their light,
My foolish, fearful heart grew wise . . .
And now, I knew that never there
I'd see again the startled hare
Or need to dread the dreams of night.

THE·EARS·OF·THE·HARE.

The Hare's Ears
by Jean de la Fontaine

The Lion, wounded by some subject's horn,
Was naturally wroth, and made decree
That all by whom such ornaments were worn
From his domains forthwith should banished be.
Bulls, Rams, and Goats at once obeyed the law:
The Deer took flight, without an hour's delay.
A timid Hare felt smitten, when he saw
The shadow of his ears, with deep dismay.
He feared that somebody, with eyes too keen,
Might call them horns, they looked so very long.
"Adieu, friend Cricket," whispered he; "I mean
To quit the place directly, right or wrong.
These ears are perilous; and, though I wore
A couple short as any Ostrich wears,
I still should run." The Cricket asked, "What for?
Such ears are only natural in Hares."
"They'll pass for horns," his frightened friend replied;
"For Unicorn's appendages, I'm sure.
And folks, if I deny it, will decide
On sending me to Bedlam, as a cure."

Night Fall in the Ti-Tree
by Geraldine Rede and Violet Teague

Night falls in the Ti-Tree,
Dusk fades from the hill—
The Frogs on their banjoes
Are strumming their fill
With a will

Banjoes in the near pond
Bones in the other—
In ecstasy Crickets
Outshrill one another
Shrill . . . Shrill . . .

The Rabbits have nibbled
Sweet grass on the furrow,
Have frisking and flirting
Loped to their burrow,
Safe on their burrow.

The Birds are all hushed now
The moon's in the sky—
Around and around us
The little Bats fly,
Waveringly

The Rabbits have nibbled
Sweet grass on the furrow,
Have frisking and flirting
Loped to their burrow,
Safe on their burrow

Are you glad, little Rabbits
To have played yet a day?
Does no foresight show you
What may happen some day?
Wellaway!

For commonest, direst,
Of wild folk's mishaps
Is to find yourselves caught in
Man's merciless traps—
Devil's own snaps

They set them and lay them
In your very door,
Then craftily strew them
With sand and leaves o'er,
Craftily o'er

You step out unwitting,
Bright moon inviting—
Ah! What a spring when
You taste its fierce biting;
Steel chain affrighting,

You scream in your anguish,
A mute thing by kind!
You make but the search easy
When Death comes to find,
O easily find!

Yet God was on your side,
Else why did He make
Such long ears to hearken?
Such bright eyes to wake?

And so, little Rabbits,
In danger some day,
Remember Who's for you,
Flirt tails and away!

Song in Autumn
by Djuna Barnes

The wind comes down before the creeping night
And you, my love, are hid within the green
Long grasses; and the dusk steals up between
Each leaf, as through the shadow quick with fright
The startled hare leaps up and out of sight.

The hedges whisper in their loaded boughs
Where warm birds slumber, pressing wing to wing,
All pulsing faintly, like a muted string
Above us where we weary of our vows—
And hidden underground the soft moles drowse.

The Town Rabbit in the Country
by Camilla Doyle

Three hours ago in Seven Dials
She lived awaiting all the trials
That haunt her race, but now shall be
Freed on the lawn to play with me.

In the dim shop her eyes were grey
And languid; but in this bright day
To a full circle each dilates,
And turns the blue of Worcester plates
In the unaccustomed sun; she stares
At strange fresh leaves; the passing airs,
Outstretching from her box's brink,
She gulps as if her nose could drink.

Now o'er the edge she scrambles slow,
Too pleased to know which way to go —
Half dazed with pleasure she explores
This sunny, eatable out-of-doors.

Then shakes and tosses up her ears
Like plumes upon bold cavaliers —
The dust flies out as catherine-wheels
Throw sparks as round she twirls and reels —
Her spine it quivers like an eel's —
Over her head she flings her heels,
Comes down askew, then waltzes till
She must reverse or else feel ill —

Reverses, then lies down and pants
As one who has no further wants,
Staring with half-believing eyes
Like souls that wake in Paradise.

Gathering Leaves
by Robert Frost

Spades take up leaves
No better than spoons,
And bags full of leaves
Are light as balloons.

I make a great noise
Of rustling all day
Like rabbit and deer
Running away.

But the mountains I raise
Elude my embrace,
Flowing over my arms
And into my face.

I may load and unload
Again and again
Till I fill the whole shed,
And what have I then?

Next to nothing for weight,
And since they grew duller
From contact with earth,
Next to nothing for color.

Next to nothing for use,
But a crop is a crop,
And who's to say where
The harvest shall stop?

Epitaph on a Hare
by William Cowper

Here lies, whom hound did ne'er pursue,
Nor swifter greyhound follow,
Whose foot ne'er tainted morning dew,
Nor ear heard huntsman's halloo;

Old Tiney, surliest of his kind,
Who, nursed with tender care,
And to domestic bounds confined,
Was still a wild Jack hare.

Though duly from my hand he took
His pittance every night,
He did it with a jealous look,
And, when he could, would bite.

His diet was of wheaten bread
And milk, and oats, and straw;
Thistles, or lettuces instead,
With sand to scour his maw.

On twigs of hawthorn he regaled,
On pippins' russet peel,
And, when his juicy salads fail'd,
Sliced carrot pleased him well.

A Turkey carpet was his lawn,
Whereon he loved to bound,
To skip and gambol like a fawn,
And swing his rump around.

His frisking was at evening hours,
For then he lost his fear,
But most before approaching showers,
Or when a storm drew near.

Eight years and five round rolling moons
He thus saw steal away,
Dozing out all his idle noons,
And every night at play.

I kept him for his humour's sake,
For he would oft beguile
My heart of thoughts that made it ache,
And force me to a smile.

But now beneath this walnut shade
He finds his long last home,
And waits, in snug concealment laid,
Till gentler Puss shall come.

He, still more aged, feels the shocks,
From which no care can save,
And, partner once of Tiney's box,
Must soon partake his grave.

On Seeing a Wounded Hare Limp by Me, Which a Fellow Had Just Shot At
by Robert Burns

Inhuman man! curse on thy barb'rous art,
And blasted be thy murder-aiming eye;
May never pity soothe thee with a sigh,
Nor never pleasure glad thy cruel heart!

Go live, poor wanderer of the wood and field,
The bitter little that of life remains;
No more the thickening brakes and verdant plains
To thee shall home, or food, or pastime yield.

Seek, mangled wretch, some place of wonted rest,
No more of rest, but now thy dying bed!
The sheltering rushes whistling o'er thy head,
The cold earth with thy bloody bosom prest.

Oft as by winding Nith I, musing, wait
The sober eve, or hail the chearful dawn,
I'll miss thee sporting o'er the dewy lawn,
And curse the ruffian's aim, and mourn thy hapless fate.

Resolution and Independence
by William Wordsworth

There was a roaring in the wind all night;
The rain came heavily and fell in floods;
But now the sun is rising calm and bright;
The birds are singing in the distant woods;
Over his own sweet voice the Stock-dove broods;
The Jay makes answer as the Magpie chatters;
And all the air is filled with pleasant noise of waters.

All things that love the sun are out of doors;
The sky rejoices in the morning's birth;
The grass is bright with rain-drops;—on the moors
The hare is running races in her mirth;
And with her feet she from the plashy earth
Raises a mist, that, glittering in the sun,
Runs with her all the way, wherever she doth run.

I was a Traveller then upon the moor;
I saw the hare that raced about with joy;
I heard the woods and distant waters roar;
Or heard them not, as happy as a boy:
The pleasant season did my heart employ:
My old remembrances went from me wholly;
And all the ways of men, so vain and melancholy.

But, as it sometimes chanceth, from the might
Of joys in minds that can no further go,
As high as we have mounted in delight
In our dejection do we sink as low;
To me that morning did it happen so;

And fears and fancies thick upon me came;
Dim sadness—and blind thoughts, I knew not, nor could name.

I heard the sky-lark warbling in the sky;
And I bethought me of the playful hare:
Even such a happy Child of earth am I;
Even as these blissful creatures do I fare;
Far from the world I walk, and from all care;
But there may come another day to me—
Solitude, pain of heart, distress, and poverty.

My whole life I have lived in pleasant thought,
As if life's business were a summer mood;
As if all needful things would come unsought
To genial faith, still rich in genial good;
But how can He expect that others should
Build for him, sow for him, and at his call
Love him, who for himself will take no heed at all?

I thought of Chatterton, the marvellous Boy,
The sleepless Soul that perished in his pride;
Of Him who walked in glory and in joy
Following his plough, along the mountain-side:
By our own spirits are we deified:
We Poets in our youth begin in gladness;
But thereof come in the end despondency and madness.

Now, whether it were by peculiar grace,
A leading from above, a something given,
Yet it befell that, in this lonely place,
When I with these untoward thoughts had striven,
Beside a pool bare to the eye of heaven
I saw a Man before me unawares:
The oldest man he seemed that ever wore grey hairs.

As a huge stone is sometimes seen to lie
Couched on the bald top of an eminence;
Wonder to all who do the same espy,
By what means it could thither come, and whence;
So that it seems a thing endued with sense:
Like a sea-beast crawled forth, that on a shelf
Of rock or sand reposeth, there to sun itself;

Such seemed this Man, not all alive nor dead,
Nor all asleep—in his extreme old age:
His body was bent double, feet and head
Coming together in life's pilgrimage;
As if some dire constraint of pain, or rage
Of sickness felt by him in times long past,
A more than human weight upon his frame had cast.

Himself he propped, limbs, body, and pale face,
Upon a long grey staff of shaven wood:
And, still as I drew near with gentle pace,
Upon the margin of that moorish flood
Motionless as a cloud the old Man stood,
That heareth not the loud winds when they call,
And moveth all together, if it move at all.

At length, himself unsettling, he the pond
Stirred with his staff, and fixedly did look
Upon the muddy water, which he conned,
As if he had been reading in a book:
And now a stranger's privilege I took;
And, drawing to his side, to him did say,
"This morning gives us promise of a glorious day."

A gentle answer did the old Man make,
In courteous speech which forth he slowly drew:

And him with further words I thus bespake,
"What occupation do you there pursue?
This is a lonesome place for one like you."
Ere he replied, a flash of mild surprise
Broke from the sable orbs of his yet-vivid eyes.

His words came feebly, from a feeble chest,
But each in solemn order followed each,
With something of a lofty utterance drest—
Choice word and measured phrase, above the reach
Of ordinary men; a stately speech;
Such as grave Livers do in Scotland use,
Religious men, who give to God and man their dues.

He told, that to these waters he had come
To gather leeches, being old and poor:
Employment hazardous and wearisome!
And he had many hardships to endure:
From pond to pond he roamed, from moor to moor;
Housing, with God's good help, by choice or chance;
And in this way he gained an honest maintenance.

The old Man still stood talking by my side;
But now his voice to me was like a stream
Scarce heard; nor word from word could I divide;
And the whole body of the Man did seem
Like one whom I had met with in a dream;
Or like a man from some far region sent,
To give me human strength, by apt admonishment.

My former thoughts returned: the fear that kills;
And hope that is unwilling to be fed;
Cold, pain, and labour, and all fleshly ills;
And mighty Poets in their misery dead.

—Perplexed, and longing to be comforted,
My question eagerly did I renew,
"How is it that you live, and what is it you do?"

He with a smile did then his words repeat;
And said that, gathering leeches, far and wide
He travelled; stirring thus about his feet
The waters of the pools where they abide.
"Once I could meet with them on every side;
But they have dwindled long by slow decay;
Yet still I persevere, and find them where I may."

While he was talking thus, the lonely place,
The old Man's shape, and speech—all troubled me:
In my mind's eye I seemed to see him pace
About the weary moors continually,
Wandering about alone and silently.
While I these thoughts within myself pursued,
He, having made a pause, the same discourse renewed.

And soon with this he other matter blended,
Cheerfully uttered, with demeanour kind,
But stately in the main; and, when he ended,
I could have laughed myself to scorn to find
In that decrepit Man so firm a mind.
"God," said I, "be my help and stay secure;
I'll think of the Leech-gatherer on the lonely moor!"

The Hare and the Frogs
by Jean de la Fontaine

One day sat dreaming in his form a Hare,
(And what but dream could one do there?)
With melancholy much perplexed
(With grief this creature's often vexed).
"People with nerves are to be pitied,
And often with their dumps are twitted;
Can't even eat, or take their pleasure;
Ennui," he said, "torments their leisure.
See how I live: afraid to sleep,
My eyes all night I open keep.
'Alter your habits,' some one says;
But Fear can never change its ways:
In honest faith shrewd folks can spy,
That men have fear as well as I."
Thus the Hare reasoned; so he kept
Watch day and night, and hardly slept;
Doubtful he was, uneasy ever;
A breath, a shadow, brought a fever.
It was a melancholy creature,
The veriest coward in all nature;
A rustling leaf alarmed his soul,
He fled towards his secret hole.
Passing a pond, the Frogs leaped in,
Scuttling away through thick and thin,
To reach their dark asylums in the mud.
"Oh! oh!" said he, "then I can make them scud
As men make me; my presence scares
Some people too! Why, they're afraid of Hares!

I have alarmed the camp, you see.
Whence comes this courage? Tremble when I come;
I am a thunderbolt of war, may be;
My footfall dreadful as a battle drum!"

There's no poltroon, be sure, in any place,
But he can find a poltroon still more base.

The Easter Bunny
by M. Josephine Todd

There's a story quite funny,
About a toy bunny,
And the wonderful things she can do;
Every bright Easter morning,
Without warning,
She colors eggs, red, green, or blue.

Some she covers with spots,
Some with quaint little dots,
And some with strange mixed colors, too
— Red and green, blue and yellow,
But each unlike its fellow
Are eggs of every hue.

And it's odd, as folks say,
That on no other day
In all of the whole year through,
Does this wonderful bunny,
So busy and funny,
Color eggs of every hue.

If this story you doubt
She will soon find you out,
And what do you think she will do?
On the next Easter morning
She'll bring you without warning,
Those eggs of every hue.

Made in the USA
Middletown, DE
21 February 2025

71634758R00052